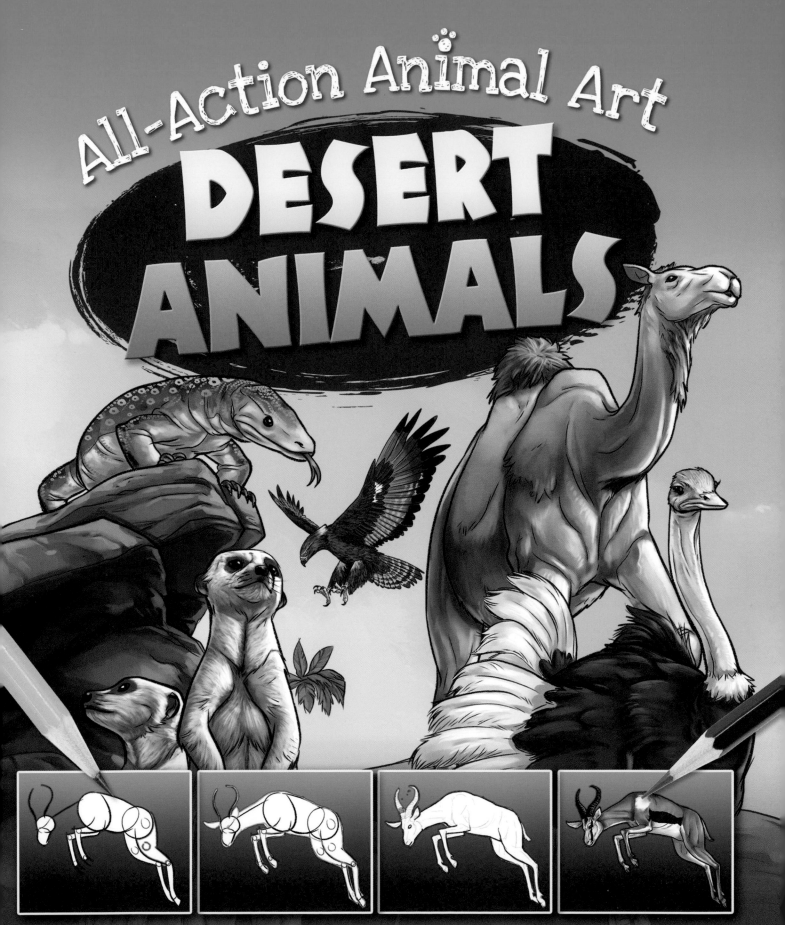

All-Action Animal Art
DESERT ANIMALS

PowerKiDS
press

Juan Calle & William Potter

Published in 2019 by **The Rosen Publishing Group, Inc.**
29 East 21st Street, New York, NY 10010

Cataloging-in-Publication Data

Names: Calle, Juan. | Potter, William.
Title: Desert animals / Juan Calle and William Potter.
Description: New York : PowerKids Press, 2019. | Series: All-action animal art | Includes glossary and index.
Identifiers: ISBN 9781538347287 (pbk.) | ISBN 9781538347300 (library bound) | ISBN 9781538347294 (6pack)
Subjects: LCSH: Desert animals in art--Juvenile literature. | Drawing--Technique--Juvenile literature.
Classification: LCC NC783.8.D47 C355 2019 | DDC 743.6--dc23

Copyright © Arcturus Holdings Ltd, 2019

Art by Juan Calle, Color by Luis Suarez (Liberum Donum)
Text by William Potter
Edited by Joe Harris and Sebastian Rydberg, with Julia Adams
Designed by Emma Randall

Manufactured in the United States of America

CPSIA Compliance Information: Batch CWPK19: For Further Information contact Rosen Publishing, New York, New York at 1-800-237-9932.

CONTENTS

GETTING STARTED

THE STEPS

The steps in this book show how you can draw a realistic animal starting with simple shapes, then building them up to form bodies before adding detail, such as horns, claws, and fur.

WHAT YOU NEED

To follow the steps in this book, all you need is some paper, a pencil (with sharpener), an eraser, paintbrushes, and water-based paints.

The first two steps show the basic building blocks—circles, ovals, and lines—that sketch out the relative sizes of the head and body, plus the positions of the limbs.

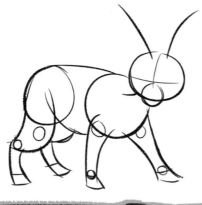

The third step shows how these simple shapes form the frame of a body. New lines are in blue as a guide. When you have drawn these outlines, you can erase the working lines you drew in steps 1 and 2.

Later steps refine the shapes and add extra detail, such as skin texture, fingers, and toes.

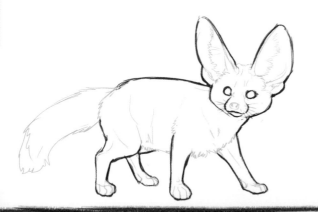

Finally, the artwork is painted, with shadows and highlights adding a three-dimensional quality.

WORLD OF WILDLIFE

This book will not only show you how to draw some incredible animals—it will inspire you to get creative!

Once you've mastered the creatures in this book, you can look beyond its pages to seek out other wildlife.

You don't have to go on a jungle or desert expedition to find subjects for sketching. You can find animals on your doorstep and in parks and zoos. You can also draw pets, of course. Once you get good at drawing a pet cat, you can use your skills to sketch big cats, such as lions and tigers.

Photos, wildlife TV shows, and nature books are also great sources of animal reference, but nothing beats drawing living, breathing, creatures. Just get out there, carry a sketchbook and pencils, and start doodling amazing creatures in the wild!

DROMEDARY

The fat in a camel's hump helps it survive for months without food.

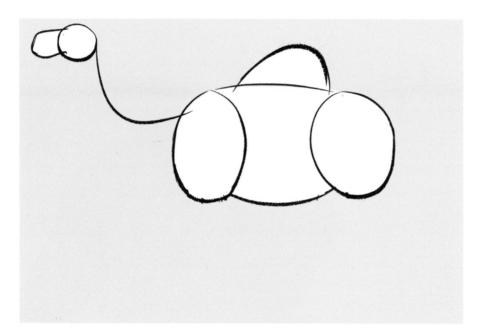

1. Start with a rounded body with a single hump. Add a head, attached to a long, curved neck.

2. Add four long, slender legs and mark the joints with small circles. Draw two lines on the face to help position the eyes.

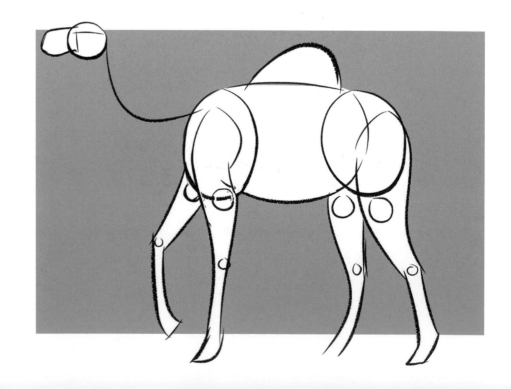

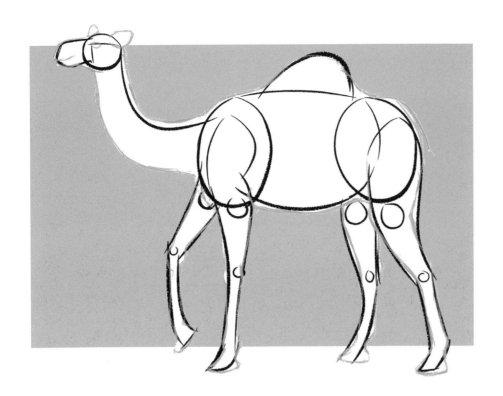

3. Give the neck thickness. Mark the position of the eyes, mouth, and tail. Add a pair of rounded ears.

4. Outline the shaggy, thicker fur below the head and over the shoulders. Draw the tail.

5. Paint the dromedary in rusty shades, using shorter brushstrokes on the thicker fur to show its texture.

Thicker fur below the dromedary's head and over its shoulders hangs down in layers. Use zigzag lines to illustrate these.

JERBOA

This far-leaping desert rodent's back legs are four times longer than its front legs.

1. Draw a bean-shaped body with a small head and larger ears.

2. Add long, jointed legs and a curved tail.

3. Thicken the neck and tail, draw the eye in position, and outline the jerboa's toes.

4. Draw a tuft on the end of the tail, plus a nose and whiskers on the head. Add fur to the body.

WILD FACT!
When chased by predators, this mouse-sized animal can leap nearly 10 feet (3 m)!

5. Paint the jerboa with light brown and cream fur. The nose, front paws, legs, and tail should be dark pink.

OSTRICH

The world's largest bird cannot fly, but it is a fast runner. It has a long neck and legs, plus lots of feathers.

1. Sketch an egg-shaped body with a long, curved neck leading to a small head and beak. Outline the wings.

2. Add two long, slender legs and use circles to mark the joints. Draw lines where the tail grows.

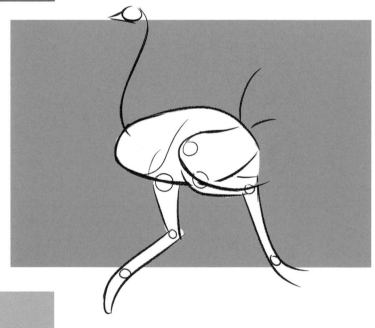

3. The neck should be as thick as the legs.

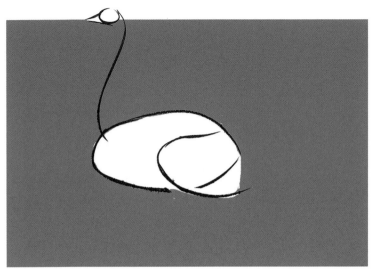

4. Add detail to the feathers, with a tuft at the bottom of the neck and a showy tail. The feet have one large and one small toe.

TOP TIP

As it runs, the ostrich's legs bend all the way back toward the body before stretching forward.

5. The neck and legs are painted pink. Use soft brushstrokes to give the feathers a fluffy finish.

SPRINGBOK

This southern African antelope leaps into the air in an action called pronking.

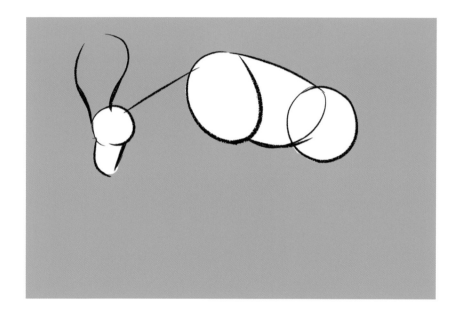

1. Build a leaping body from two joined circles. Add a neck and head with two curved horns.

2. Sketch bent front legs and stretched back legs. Mark the leg joints with circles. Draw a line along the head to help position the eye.

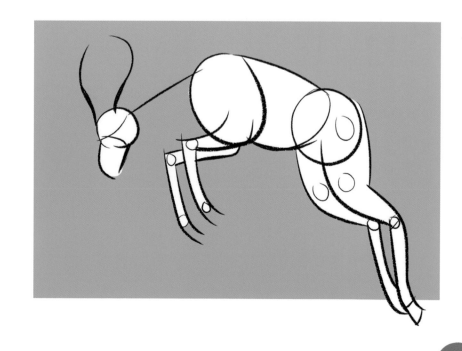

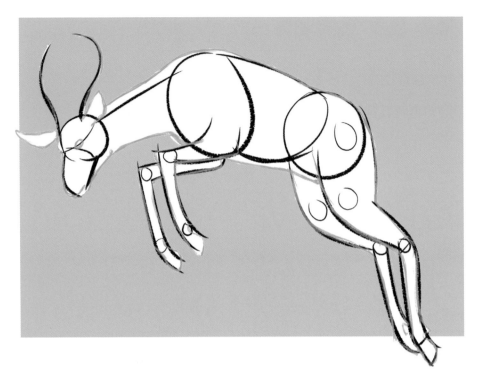

3. Thicken the neck, and draw the eye and two ears in position. Flatten the shape of the belly.

4. Shape the horns with ringed markings. Draw the mouth, hooves, and tail. Add lines for the muscles on the body.

When a springbok pronks, it pushes up with its back legs, raises its rear half, then lands on its front legs.

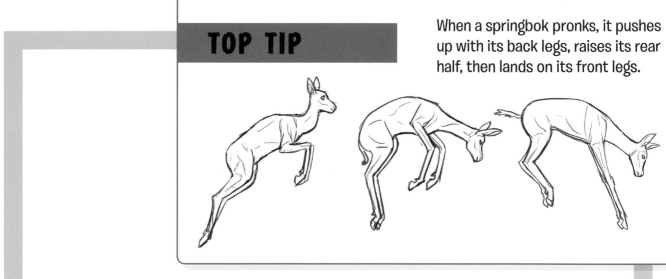

5. Paint the springbok with a rusty back and legs, white underside, and a brown stripe on the face and side.

MEERKAT

This sociable African animal stands upright on guard duty, watching out for predators on land or in the air.

1. Draw an upright body built from two rough circles, and add an oval head.

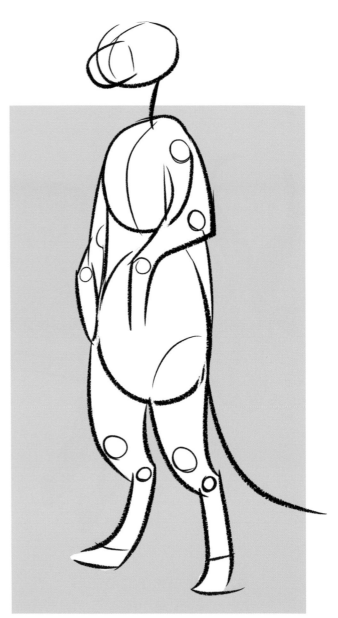

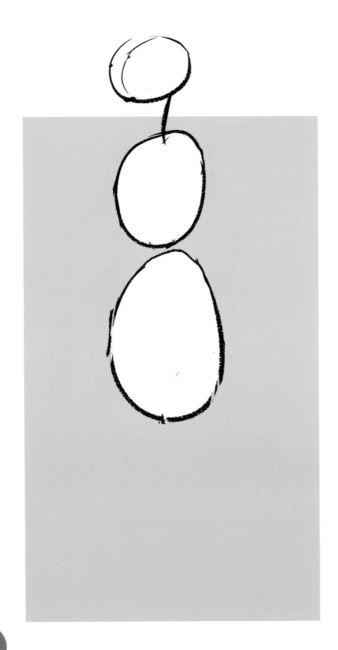

2. Connect the two body circles. The meerkat has bent arms and legs, plus a tail at the rear, used for balance. Mark the joints with circles, and add a snout to the face.

3. Add thickness to the neck and tail. Draw the eyes and an ear. Shape the long, clawed paws.

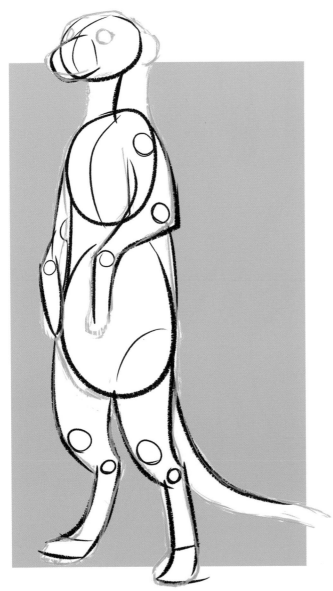

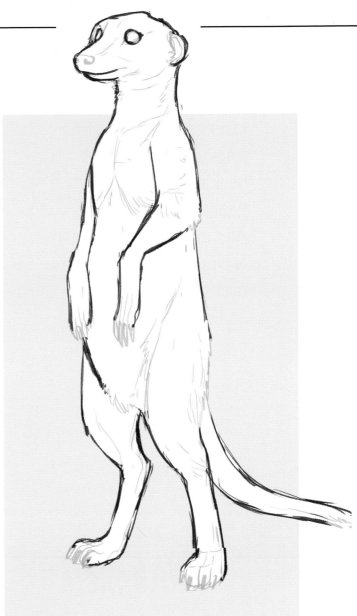

4. Draw a nose. Add rough fur lines under the chin, over the chest, and where the top of the legs meet the belly.

5. The front of the meerkat is white with smoky shadows. The back and top of the head are pale brown. Add a dark brown patch around the eyes and over the ears, nose, and claws.

WILD FACT!

Meerkats are immune to scorpion poison and will happily snack on these stinging creatures.

GULDEN EAGLE

This high-flying raptor swoops
to grab prey in its sharp talons.

1. Start with a long, oval
body, short neck, rounded
head, and curved beak.

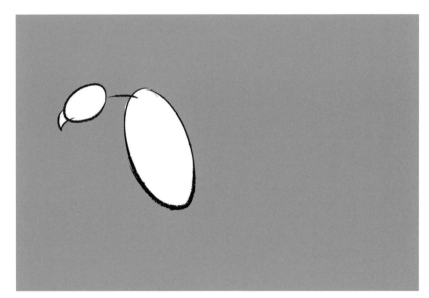

2. Add pointed legs
with feet and two
spreading wings.
Sketch the outline of
the tail feathers.

3. Outline a fan shape on the tail and an eye, then start drawing the individual feathers on the wings.

4. The eagle has three distinct layers of feathers on its wings. Add a hint of feathers on the chest, plus more on its legs.

5. Paint the eagle in shades of brown with patches of white, black, and tan. Then, add dark brown smudges for a feathery effect.

SCORPION

The eight-legged scorpion has two large pincers and a barbed tail with a venomous stinger.

1. Start with a round head and sausage-shaped body.

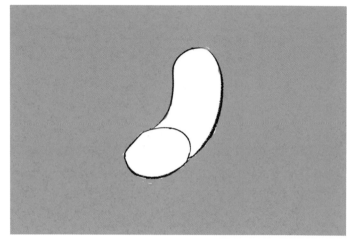

2. Add a curved tail on the rear, then draw eight legs and two arms to the front section.

3. The tail is made up of five bumpy sections, plus the stinger. Shape the legs and arms, then draw the mouthparts on the head.

4. Divide the arms, legs, tail, and arched back into sections. Add the sharp pincers and two dots for the eyes.

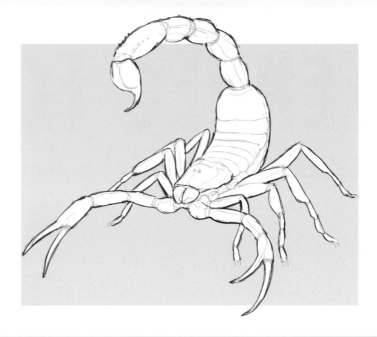

TOP TIP

The scorpion's pincer arms are divided into clear sections with tiny hairs. The pincers have a serrated inside edge.

5. Paint the scorpion in golden shades with patches of brown and pale highlights to show its shiny finish. The stinger has a red tip.

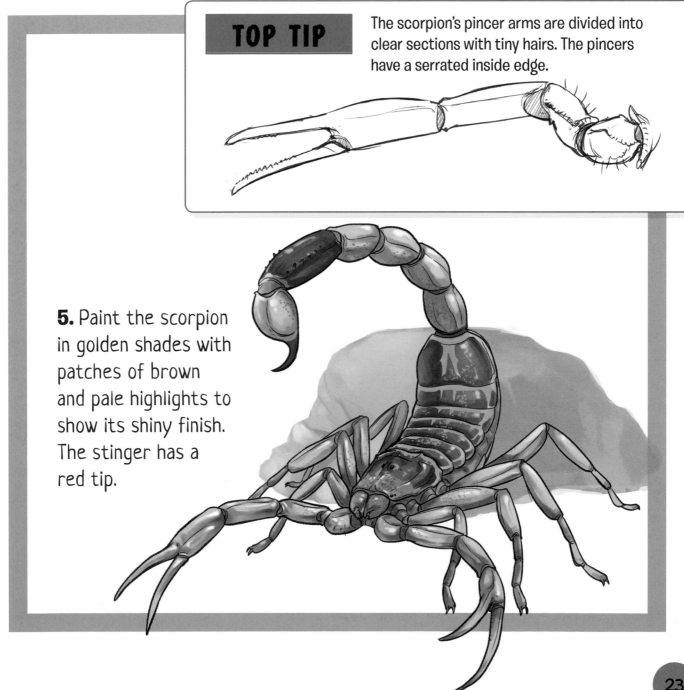

FENNEC FOX

The world's smallest fox has some of the largest ears.

1. Join two circles for a body, and add a round head.

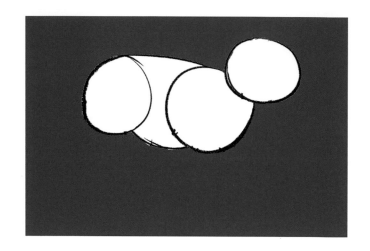

2. The front legs are straight, and the back legs are curved. Use circles to mark the joints. Add a snout and a line to position the eyes. Two upward strokes mark the ears.

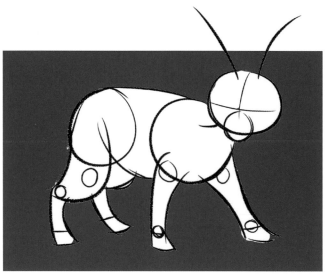

3. Outline the fox's two ears, which are shaped like wings. Position the eyes, and add a curve to the rear.

4. Draw a bushy tail, paws, and a furry belly. Give the fox a nose and whiskers, plus some fur lines inside the ears.

5. Paint the fox with short brushstrokes, creating patches of orange and silvery white. Add a chocolate-brown tail tip and a hint of pink inside the ears.

WILD FACT!
The fennec fox's large ears help it stay cool in the desert by radiating the animal's body heat.

MONITOR LIZARD

This powerful lizard crawls over the sand, searching for food by tasting the air with its tongue.

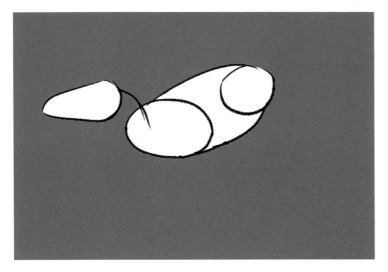

1. Connect two circles to form an egg-shaped body. Add a neck and a long, pointed head.

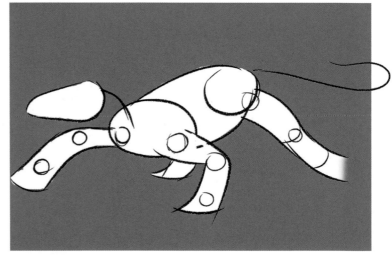

2. Draw four widely spaced, thick legs with circles to mark the joints. Add a tail like a snake.

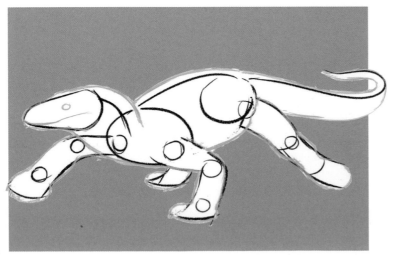

3. Draw an eye and mouth, plus the outline of the body. Add a thick neck and tail, plus rounded feet.

4. Add sharp claws to the feet, a forked tongue from the mouth, and creases on the lizard's skin.

5. Paint the lizard a pale tan, then add a darker brown "drip" pattern over its head, back, tail, and legs. Leave out a few spots across the back.

WILD FACT!
The monitor lizard has venomous saliva, which helps kill its prey when it bites.

RATTLESNAKE

Watch your step! This venomous snake is primed to strike!

1. Draw a long, curving line for the snake's body, with an open mouth at one end.

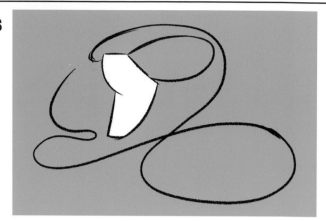

2. Add the jaw lines and fangs to the mouth, and a rough rectangle to the other end of the body.

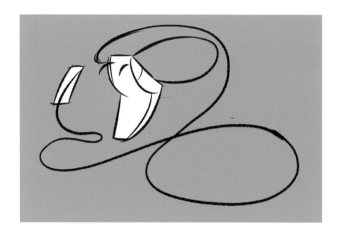

3. Draw two curved fangs in the snake's mouth. Add thickness to the curving line for the snake's body.

4. Sketch a pattern of crossing lines over the snake. Divide the rattle at the end of the tail into sections. Add detail inside the open mouth.

Close up, the snake's skin is made up of scales of different shades. These build up into a pattern of diamonds over its body.

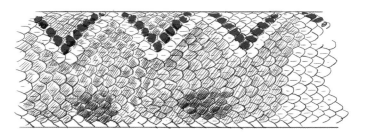

5. Carefully paint a diamond pattern over the snake's body in shades of brown and white. Paint the inside of the mouth pink.

GLOSSARY

barbed Having a sharp point that is difficult to remove.

immune Resistant to something, such as poison.

poison A substance that can cause illness or death when it is breathed in or swallowed.

predator An animal that hunts and kills other animals for food.

pronk When a springbok or an antelope leaps in the air with an arched back and straight legs.

rodent A type of mammal that has incisors (front teeth) that grow throughout its life. Rodents gnaw to regulate the length of their incisors.

serrated Having a jagged edge.

sociable To enjoy being in the company of others.

talon The claw of a bird of prey.

tuft A collection or bunch of something, such as feathers.

venomous Able to inject a toxic substance into another creature, such as by biting or stinging it.

fURtHeR INfoRMATIoN

Books:

Ames, Lee J. *Draw 50 Endangered Animals*. New York, NY: Watson–Guptill, 2013.

Chambers, Ailin. *Animals*. New York, NY: Gareth Stevens Publishing, 2015.

Cuddy, Robbin. *Learn to Draw Zoo Animals*. Lake Forest, CA: Walter Foster Jr., 2016.

Davis, Rich. *The 1-Minute Artist: Learn How to Draw Almost Anything in 6 Easy Steps*. New York, NY: Race Point Publishing, 2016.

Gray, Peter. *Everyone Can Draw Animals*. New York, NY: Windmill Books, 2013.

Websites:

PowerKids Press has developed an online list of websites related to the subject of this book. This site is updated regularly. Please use this link to access the list: www.powerkidslinks.com/aaaa/desertanimals

INDEX